MW00583551

IN A WORLD OF CONSCIOUSNESS

IN A **WORLD** OF CONSCIOUSNESS

THE WORDS OF
RAVEN BROOKS

Copyright © 2021 Raven Brooks

All rights reserved. No part of this publication may be
reproduced, distributed, or transmitted in any form or by
any means, including photocopying, recording, or other
electronic or mechanical methods, without prior written
permission of the author.

First Edition March 2021
Printed in the United States of America
ISBN: 978-0578876399

Cover Design by Jeff Crosby
Book Design by Maureen Cutajar

Published by Taylor Publishing Group
www.taylorpublishinggrp.com

To my precious mother, Sandy Davis Brooks.
Thank you, Mama, for unconditionally loving me
and always reminding me of my gifts.

—∽—

I would like to thank everyone who believed in this project before it came to life. Thank you for encouraging me to write a book, thank you for the promise of ordering my book, and thank you for helping me to manifest my dream.

Contents

LIONESS,

Play in the shadows.
Femininity is dark; it's where your powers are set free.
Release the beast.
Then tame her.
She's not meant for those who run from her.
Don't be afraid. Chaotic is good.
Black can be bitter but sweet will illude.
Breathe Lioness. Let her run free.
Your shadow reflects you, eye, and me.

06/14/19
WILD-CHILD,

You've been drained before.
Now you water those who water you.
Stay charged.
Connect with those who empower you.
Your energy is infinite when allowed by you.
Your energy is soaring you'll soon fly too.
Aligned with yourself, you attract you.
Energies around became rocket fuel.
Dismiss the vampires. You are no fool.
Wild-Child, you're wild and your energy is your tool.

06/17/19
SOURCE,

You are the finish line.
What are you searching for?
All is within.
Your path is not linear.
There is no end goal.
Your path is cyclical.
Infinite.
Infinity.
Deliberately slow unwanted momentum.
Meditate.
Tap in.
Bring forth all you are meant to.

06/18/19
BLAH,

What's normal anyway?
I'm moving in an unapologetic way.
Loving all of me and all the things that I create.
Embodying the magic of the least traveled way.
My path of least resistance is a path that is so new.
My path is calling out to me, I chose to live my truth.
My universe is unique to me; unique to you.
Inspired by what's different so I'll be different too.
Source, I've realized it is me you're living through.
I'm so powerful, enchanted, and galactic too.
It's starting to dawn on me what that magic really do.
I've tapped in and I don't have one thing to prove.

SMILE,

It takes more muscles to frown.
In this magical reality why choose to be down?
Living life with the midas;
All that I touch is gold.
I stop and smell the flowers as the greatness unfolds.
Laughing at negativity.
Because I know it ain't touching me.
I'm attracting so much love because I spend my time loving
  me.
All my people are one with me.
We are rising collectively.
Expanding our minds and increasing expectancies.
Dwelling in positivity.
Raising our Kundalini.
Meditating on our needs and our wants come so easy.

06/20/19
MOCHA,

Your essence is so pure.
Allow yourself the freedom to respect what you endure.
Please respect your temple. When you know better it shows.
When the energy is off, you are guaranteed to know.
We must move without words. Vibrations take the lead.
And wishy-washy motives can be seen more easily.
Be open to your dreamworld. Work with your inner guides.
Let the spirit of the Raven come and teach you how to fly.
Let the Lion teach you strength and protection of your
    Pride.
Endurance leads to treasure so stay strong for the ride.
The ugly doesn't phase you. Unconditional is the way.
The love is only true when the love is here to stay.
Mocha, mocha, mocha. Be strong, yet sweet.
And don't forget to dive into the blackness underneath.

EYE,

Am a window of consciousness,
Just as eyes are windows to the soul.
The marathon continues it is not a race,
Less rushing brings tranquil to the soul.
If Eye let myself just be and enjoy the ride
Oh the places Eye Am allowed to go.
Exploring my reality is truly wild,
Eye Am seeing as above, so below.
The Summer Solstice has arrived
Now Eye look back and see
That in Winter months Eye died,
Then Spring birthed a new me.
The Spring brought time to cultivate
And prepare for harvesting
And now that Summer months are here.
The Raven can fly free.

EGO,

The world is our mirror.
Let's look our reflection deep into the eye.
What have you attracted?
Have you recognized why?
I am happy, my love, that you are not afraid.
If you can't look at yourself, are you showing your true face?
Have you faced the truth?
Who is your shadow?
She knows all the things you subconsciously expose.
Get to know her. Then choose to let her be.
Within the shadows you will see, the truth will set you free.
In the dark you'll find the light.
The spark will burst to flames.
The dark won't seem so dark and you won't see life the same.
Those things that brought you fear.
Become a fun part of the game.
You'll break through the barrier,
And truly fly away.
Your shadow will show you
How to set yourself free
And then you will be face to face
With the new and truer me.

SHADOW,

This is us.
What is up?
How you gone act when they play with ya?
What is life?
What is love?
Either way, you have the power to
Vibrate high
To let it be
To let it go and soon they will see,
Play with me.
Play yourself.
Karma raises hell if you take her there.
And listen here,
To what I say.
My energy's pure; concentrate.
So, if you want
Gone 'head and play.
When you get yours, you'll be blown away.

07/02/19
DARK,

I was once afraid but now I embrace you.
My inability to see has forced me to feel.
I no longer wonder with logic what's real.
I'm water. I flow.
Currently the current is stripping my soul.
My soul is complex; there's layers to peel.
The deeper I go the more I reveal.
I'm granted with peace and serenity.
As I discover more of me.
So much love in vulnerability.
I'm unconditionally loving me.

07/03/19
NIGHT,

The cosmos are speaking.
Lately I've been feeling so dreamy.
Clearly, I've reached a new level
Because I can't help but live my life lucidly.
My mind is creating reality.
My time is not spent childishly.
I've walked into a new paradigm.
And this is happening constantly.
Forever changing... and disengaging.
In all that is less than amazing
I've placed myself on a pedestal.
It's rising higher and higher up lately.
No longer a victim. I saved me.
No longer lacking. I'm raging.
Not here to play. I'm here to stay.
I'm fire. A flame, Trailblazing.

GODDESS,

You are expanding. Take a look around.
What surrounds you now?
The old you has died.
You've realigned.
Burned bridges light the way.
Meditate and paint the day.
Your inner fire burns away so you're brighter day by day.
Fear no longer consumes you.
It amuses you.
You see the opportunity of diving into the newer you.
It's true that soon, you will be new again.
So, BE in the moment; appreciate the NOW within.
Crying ain't a sin but a cleanse.
Release and cry again.
Your tears are elixir.
Inducing self-love on the mixer.
Alchemy.
I chose to be.
Me.

MAGICK,

You are the power. Bend your reality as you please.

Please, take each hour and learn your pleasures.

Pleasure yourself and let resistance go free.

Freedom is key. Birds don't belong in cages; they'll always
sing.

Singing in bondage creates the illusion of leisure.

But leisure in confinement brings an internal bleed.

Bleeding in spirit; withering away.

Away your mind goes to another place.

Place your freedom in your heart and release yourself from
this cage.

Your magic does not belong in a box.

Open it. If it's closed, you won't find your way.

07/08/19
LOVE,

Rediscovery is bittersweet.
New worlds open up.
Reevaluate certain things.
Preconceived notions hold you up.
Readjust; things must leave.
Eye will resist nothing.
Realizing eye receive.
All eye manifest is coming.
Reflecting on my peace.
Leaves me feeling euphoric.
Rebooting my mind;
So, eye will get more of it.
Realized Eye Am alive,
When my passions erupted.
Release so eye will rise.
Use passion to create something.
Retreat into my mind
Eye do not want for nothing.
Regenerate my life
Dying and rebirthing
Refreshing is nice
Eye have been feeling so lovely.
Now eye am realigned
And eye regret nothing.

SPIRIT,

My cups runs over.
Overflowing with abundance.
I'm overcoming. I run this.
I'm creating my reality. I decided to become it.
My God. You have risen within me.
Oh my, I feel the Kundalini.
Uncoiled and moving.
This dimension is so soothing.
I found the God within and dismissed all illusions.
No longer feel the need to jump to conclusions.
No longer beg and plead for resistance or delusion
I took a ride with me; she was pleased to see me grooving.
Dancing to my own song.
I asked her if she'd sing along.
No such thing as getting words wrong,
When you know it's right where you belong.
Locked and loaded.
I have remolded.
The old me is gone. That chapter is closing.
And once it closed a new door sprung open.
Opportunities calling, reaching out, and provoking
A better me
So readily,
Becoming all,
I'm meant to be.
So steadily,

Addressing the,
Shadows that are,
A part of me.
What will it be,
That makes me see
All the power
That resides in me?
By the hour I discover me.
I find the power by loving me.

07/17/19
WISDOM,

Space is vast.
Fine tune.
Time is fast.
Vibe through.
Delete the past.
Make new.
Memories cast,
Spells too.
You won't be last.
Stay true.
Burn the trash,
Let loose.
You're the tap,
Break through.
The miracle you want, wants you.

07/18/19
SILENCE,

No longer speak.
Hold the appearance of the things you wish to see.
Be alone in your element.
Carry yourself out to sea.
No longer aroused by the loud or phony.
Peace.
Tranquil.
Calm.
Translucent.
It is now second nature to sense the movement.
Confidence is key to unlock the intuitive.
Godfidence is free and leads a life so lucid.
Dream with eyes wide. Open to the sky.
Feeling like I died and became much more alive.
Let the God arise. My God she hears the cries.
For clarity and power so right now, I feel aligned.
So now I take a dive. I live to take the risk,
Of living in my power, may my words dismiss the mist.
The fog has gotten thick.
The faith has made me rich.
A mustard seed, forget it, I've built mountains up for this.
So, trust me when I say,
The worlds in disarray.
I notice the placeholders
And I've come to trailblaze.
My walk is so unique.

I love and I won't speak.
So please question yourself if you think to question me.

08/26/19
FEMININE,

Show them your divinity of energy.

Are you feeling me?

Because I'm feeling you as soon as you step through.

Tell me something.

Are you living in your truth?

If not, what do you plan to do?

You will never be satisfied, living to satisfy.

Others that is… Because self-satisfaction is the gift that up-
lifts.

Bless yourself with the wisdom that you give.

Apply your knowledge and watch your life shift.

Stay dedicated don't ever quit.

Learn what makes you go and what makes you tick.

Stand for something so you do not fall.

Abundance is here but you don't need it all.

Set goals and objectives so you are involved,

In the life that you dreamed of for so long.

Your power as a woman is unmatched.

Your soulful essence is that which the patriarch combats.

But a seed planted deep will be deeply rooted.

And the darkness turns to bright light that is as dense as
fluid.

Washing over you. Purity.

Dancing in the breeze with fluidity.

A flower that blossomed so beautifully.

With gangster, a light heart, and maturity.

What more could you ask for?
I walked through open doors.
Only to discover myself; my wealth.
Moving in stealth has been great for my health but no matter.
My life speaks even in the silence of my voice.
Words provoke emotion but action is a choice.
I chose to move with intention.
And like rockets I shot to a different dimension.
We are not on the same plane.
Plain and simple.
I leveled up and I smiled so hard it showed my dimples.
Sheesh.
I love my newfound peace.
I've woven together a masterpiece.
As I master peace, I find self-love.
Recognized the God in me, as below so above.

GARDEN,

Be at peace.
The fruit is the last thing to grow on the tree.
Tranquility comes as you nurture yourself.
Transformation comes with patience in each step.
Stay grounded. Focus. Get rooted in your dreams.
Allow yourself to grow by having leniency.
L's are lessons teaching how to succeed.
Wins are cultivated once you practice what you preach.
So, cultivate your truth. Water it with pride.
Be proud of what you've seeded.
Be proud watching it rise.
Be delicate and gentle.
Please enjoy the ride.
And when you start to blossom,
Do not be surprised.

09/02/19

REFLECTION,

Check your connection.
Are you in tune with your own inner sanctions?
The God in you will check you when you need it.
But are you close enough to yourself to feel it?
G check time. Get yourself realigned. You've been feeling
so high on this rollercoaster ride.
You're on the peak and no longer feel weak.
When you drop down in recessions,
Ain't no depression.
Instead something clicks,
Hard times ain't slick
You can't be knocked out when you know what it is.
You know what you want.
You manifested this.
Be careful what you wish
There's work that comes with it.
Always put that work in.
Life is a consistent win
When L's are lessons
Wins are blessings.
Create your own miracles
They're searching for you.
Consistency creates magic, That's the universal truth.

PERSPECTIVE,

Choose what you see.
Seek what you be.
Attract who you are.
Or the opposite you'll keep.
The contrast will teach,
Exactly what you need.
And once that seeps in,
It's a new kind of free.
Put your best foot forward.
And manifest your dreams
Find yourself and moreover
Create the self that you fiend.
The true you is waiting.
It's a self-love kind of thing.
It's difficult at times but you know what you need.
Are you living your truth?
Or just talking about it?
Do you live in alignment?
Or are you living without it?
Do you water yourself first?
Or create a drought?
Tryna drown other people
While you suffer dry mouth?
You can't pour from an empty cup.
You can try if you want.
But soon enough it shows

It was all just a flaunt.

Because once you're exposed you will have to re-up.

So, do yourself a favor and fill your own cup.

TAP,

Dig deeper.
You know what you're feeling,
Turn yourself to a believer.
Once you find the source, you'll notice that the flow is gold.
Once you find the source, you'll live the greatest story ever
   told.
Experience with willingness; watch with grace. Don't over-
   load,
Yourself with wishful thinking when reality's your TV show.
Sit back and be observant,
Then tell yourself what to do.
It's up to you to listen, that's the value of being in tune.
Notice all your patterns and don't fall for the illusions.
Keep up with your pace and create growth with movement.
Change is good it brings forth evolution.
Then it hits you hard when you see what you've been doing.
Let Go. Let God. Let Love. Let Be.
Go with your flow for it begets peace.
Practice, practice, practice, practice, practice what you
   preach.
Choose not to preach out loud if it is you that you teach.
Monkey see, monkey do, monkey hear, monkey defies.
Take action with alignment, watch things shift before your
   eyes.
If it creates resistance, cut of all the ties.
And if you stay persistent soon enough you learn to fly.

SUN,

Shine bright.
Higher frequencies are calling as you gaze into the sky.
Reached nirvana and feeling alive.
Lower frequencies grounded me.
Now it's time to rise.
Looking up and moving forward.
Events around me go so fast.
Take my time and move slower.
Sit back and watch the chaos pass.
I am the eye of the storm.
All is calm here.
I'm surrounded by wild energies while my center is clear.
I look up into the vortex.
My manifestations are here.
Dreams come to me in 1...2...3.
Basking in now, what an honor to achieve,
All that I'm here for. I won't ever leave,
Myself behind. My mind is mine. My higher self is free,
To move in this dimension, my energy is cleaned,
Of all the blockages that prevent my release.
The God in me is walking. Taking one step at a time.
The Goddess has arrived, and her frequency is high.
Vibing at all energies of love and above.
She crawled, and walked, and ran so far and now it's time
  to jump.
No fear allowed. I've balanced out.

Prophecies are spoken when I open my mouth.
A medium, a channel, the source is foundation.
The universe keeps blessing me, creating elevation.
Moving on up. Higher mind. Higher vibe.
I once was just existing now I'm on a joy ride.

HIBERNATE,

In the darkest days we recreate.
The world around me began to change,
As I began to break the mental chains.
The past had this hold on me.
My power was focused on what folded on me.
But now I'm free within my soul.
And all that I touch turns into gold.
Clean. Clear. Cleansed. Collected.
This power within me must be respected.
I made the choice to make this life mine.
My entire journey became a sign.
I am the heavens. I am the earth.
The God in me knows her worth.
This cosmic concentration of life I have,
Values higher than any commodity I've ever had.
The cards I've been dealt have many gifts.
Staying consistent brings cosmic rifts.
As soon as I believe things will stay the same,
I take off like a rocket and change the game.
Love is everything and everything is love.
I crave higher vibrations, so I choose to rise above.
I teach myself the way. The guide within is real.
If God is within, whom or what shall I fear?

ABOUT THE AUTHOR

 Raven Brooks is a native of Stanley, North Carolina. She currently attends North Carolina Agricultural and Technical State University of Greensboro, NC obtaining a Bachelor of Science in Economics with a double minor in Spanish and Multimedia Journalism. Raven loves nature, writing, and creating art of all forms. Her vision is to uplift, and inspire others locally, and internationally through poetry.

Raven has loved reading and writing since she was in elementary school. In 2016, she performed at her first poetry slam. At the time, her life was dedicated to college basketball but, after her performance, she was inspired to explore more artistic pursuits. During her final college years, she began performing at various open mics, showcases, and other poetry events. From there, her love for poetry continued to grow. Throughout this journey, *In A World of Consciousness* was born.

Made in the USA
Columbia, SC
07 May 2021

36845274R00026